YOU *are* INVITED

How to Plan Everything from Intimate Gatherings to Texas-Sized Parties

REEDY PRESS

Reedy Press

PO Box 5131

St. Louis, MO 63139

www.reedypress.com

Library of Congress Control Number: 2015942721

ISBN: 978-1-68106-016-3

Design by Richard Roden

Copywriting by Danny Bonvissuto

Photography by Carmine LiDestri, Visual Image Photography

Printed in the United States

15 16 17 18 19   5 4 3 2 1

For my sister-in-law, Helen Gardner—a real and honest woman who left the party too soon.
I am forever inspired by her love of family, fierce dedication to friends,
and desire to not waste one moment of this precious life.

I miss you every day.

CONTENTS

INTRODUCTION

Party planning is my love language. Friends tell me they don't share my love of hosting events—the very idea of navigating the layers of logistics makes them overwhelmed and nervous. But very few things make me happier than channeling all the passion I feel for a cause or person into the time I spend obsessing over menus, searching out venues, and dabbling in hundreds of details.

And I'm not ashamed to say it: the excitement that bubbles up in me when I'm putting a party together is like a drug. I've become addicted to the feeling of seeing joy on guests' faces and it's a high I chase from event to event.

When I was a little girl, I loved to watch my mother set the table for company. She taught me about place settings, crystal, and where to put the butter knife. As I grew up and started entertaining in my own home, I spent hours in bookstores researching ways to throw bigger, better parties. Back then I wasn't financially able to host extravagant events, but I figured out how to make them beautiful, elegant, and fun.

These days, I go over the top because I can. But what really makes a party a "Janelle party" isn't the wow factor—it's that I keep focused on making my guests happy. From the moment they arrive, I want them to know they're being taken care of. I want everything to be easy. I want them to eat delicious food, drink great cocktails, talk, and laugh. Their pleasure is the key to a successful event, whether the budget is small or large.

I can still see myself in that bookstore years ago, looking for inspiration, and I hope this book will do for you what so many others did for me. When you start with love, laughter, and a sincere desire to give your guests a good time, it's impossible to go wrong. Entertaining doesn't have a price tag if you love it.

FOREWORD

I believe good food brings good people together. In bold flavors with no borders. I believe being present with guests—giving them a few minutes of undivided attention—makes all the difference in their experience.

I believe entertaining is an art. In keeping things casual out front and busy behind the scenes. I believe in organization, asking for help, and delegating to those I trust.

I believe in Janelle Friedman, a friend, client, and kindred spirit when it comes to planning parties. I love her warmth and humor, personality and professionalism, and ability to be in the moment, no matter what else is going on.

Janelle is a natural entertainer—it's in her bones and in her blood. Over the past twenty years I've cooked in enough of her kitchens to know how dedicated she is to her vision—from the big picture to small details—and how gracefully she navigates countless logistics to ensure each guest has the best experience possible.

Much like Janelle's legendary events, *You Are Invited* is well organized, delicious, gorgeous, and fun. Make it your bible to plan parties that guests will talk about long after they're over.

—*Dean Fearing, chef/partner of Fearing's Restaurant, author of* **The Texas Food Bible,** *and the father of Southwestern cuisine.*

ACKNOWLEDGMENTS

Though it's me you see on the cover, there are so many people just outside the frame who support me in every way, every day. A very special thank-you to:

My husband, Larry, who always keeps me on my toes. For trusting me, letting me be who I want, do what I want, and filling my life with romance and laughter.

My daughter Heather, a beautiful, caring wife, mother, and daughter. For making me a grandmother and trusting me like a friend.

My son Jason, who's grown into such a good man and great attorney. For choosing to work at the firm and letting me be a part of his life every day.

My son Brian, the unofficial "mayor of Dallas," who knows everyone and everything in town. A lawyer by education, he found his passion in the restaurant business, where every night is a party. I'm proud of him and the path he's chosen.

My son Eric, who's sweet and easygoing. I love that he always starts my day at the office with a smile and a kiss. I've always admired the fact that he's content to go at his own pace, no matter what the rest of the world is doing.

My daughter Jaclyn, who's beautiful, powerful, intelligent, and kind. Just hearing her voice on the phone makes me feel good.

My daughter Taylor, a vibrant, beautiful, intelligent, and bold woman who can command a room just by walking into it. My shopping buddy anytime.

My daughter-in-law Ilona and son-in-law Ryan for loving my children the way they do and being such kind people.

My dear friend Carol Aaron, who mentored me by example in the world of charitable causes, and my bestie Yvette Feiger, who is always my biggest cheerleader and most fun playmate.

Debbie Vaughan, who makes all the things I imagine become a reality and is my all-time best psychotic business manager.

Marketing and public relations machine Andrea Alcorn, one of the smartest, most resourceful women I know. For being such a good listener and making magic happen.

Mo, the talented artist who makes me feel as beautiful on the outside as I feel on the inside.

My family and friends in Dallas and beyond, who always show up for my events. It's never a party until you arrive.

let's get this party started

beauty is never boring

OPEN HOUSES

at Home and Work

chapter **1**

DEFINITION
Though the term is often attached to events that celebrate a new home or business, "open house" also designates the type of occasion where people can drop in anytime between designated hours. This is a great idea for events in small spaces with a big guest list—that way everyone doesn't show up at the same time.

LENGTH
Open houses should go two to three hours. Any longer and it's considered a party.

RSVP
An open house invitation should always ask guests to RSVP. Though people will come and go, you still need a head count for food and drinks.

OFF-LIMITS ROOMS
Don't let an unfinished room or area keep you from hosting an open house. Simply close the door to let guests know it's a restricted area.

CLIMATE CONTROL
Don't let the weather decide whether you show off an outdoor area. Use a see-through tent so guests get the full effect.

I've been CEO of my family's law firm for more than 27 years. My life is full of attorneys, including my husband and four of our six children. So trust me on this: There is no law that says an open house has to be boring.

They certainly have that reputation: when guests receive an invitation to celebrate a new home or business, they expect to have a drink and a handful of cocktail nuts, mill around awkwardly, and escape quickly after congratulating the host.

So blow them away. Though the purpose of an open house is to show off a space, the guests should always be the focus. And the difference between a bored guest and an impressed guest is just a little effort and imagination.

play with your food

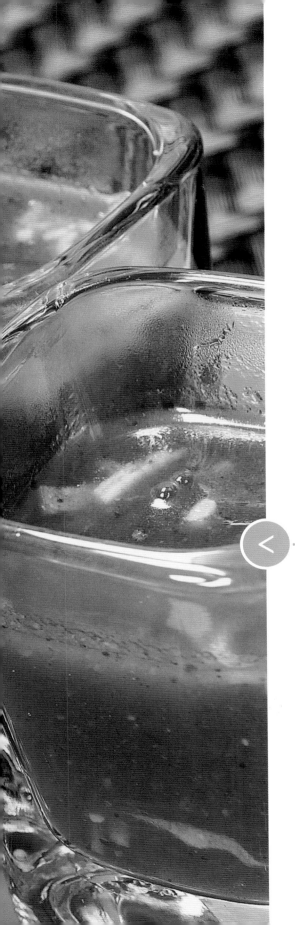

PAYING ATTENTION TO HOW FOOD IS DISPLAYED AND SERVED IS AN EASY WAY TO CREATE A MAJOR SPARK

Well thought out food adds energy and excitement, but it also draws guests in. People go where the food is—*it's Entertaining 101*—so set it up in ways that'll keep the guests moving around, exploring new areas, and interacting with other guests.

❊ Have a server walk around with a tray of cotton candy or bags of popcorn.

❊ Serve soup in shot glasses.

❊ People love a picnic: take hot dogs and hamburgers to a new level with a fun condiment bar.

❊ Is your caterer a notable chef? Have him or her pose with guests for pictures after service.

❊ Do a Mediterranean spread: cured meats, cheeses, olives, almonds, dried fruits, pita bread, and crostini.

❊ Interactive food stations are a fun way to combine entertainment and eating.

  o Hire a sushi chef to make rolls.

  o Have someone create custom omelets in the kitchen or pancakes on the patio.

  o Station a sommelier at the bar for wine and/or beer tastings.

FOOD FOR THOUGHT

MINI MENU

When my son Brian opened an event space in downtown Dallas, I had servers walk around with petite pairings—a small bite paired with a tiny drink. It's a fun way to offer a variety of foods and create energy every time a guest experiences a different selection.

Wine and cheese: comté gougères, small glass of wine

Burger and Coke: turkey and short rib sliders, 6-ounce Coke, and red bendy straw

Taco or tacos and tequila: whitefish taco, mini bottle of Patrón tequila with cork drilled to accommodate a tiny lime green straw

Pizza and beer: slice of flatbread pizza, tiny bottle of beer

FRIEDMAN & FEIGER ATTORNEYS AT LAW OPEN HOUSE MENU
CREATED BY CHEF DEAN FEARING

Passed hors d'oeuvres

❊ Smoked salmon nachos

❊ Crab salad with avocado, sweet pepper confit, shaved fennel, and smoked carrot cumin vinaigrette on cheese cracker

❊ Tortilla soup shooter

❊ Chilled sweet corn vichyssoise shooter with smoked tomatoes

❊ Grilled vegetable bruschetta with goat cheese

❊ Barbecued buffalo tacos with green chili salsa ······

❊ Smoked chicken and mango quesadillas with lime and sour cream

❊ Tiny crab cakes with spicy mustard sauce

Small plates

❊ Barbecue glazed salmon on corn whipped mashed potatoes

❊ Chili braised short ribs with wild mushroom polenta

❊ Sugarcane chicken on vegetable stir-fried rice

❊ Seared curry scallops on coconut jasmine rice

Dessert performance station

❊ Bananas foster on double chocolate brownie cake with vanilla bean ice cream

KNOCK, KNOCK.
GUEST SATISFACTION STARTS
AT THE FRONT DOOR

No matter how many lamb lollipops you've made or signature cocktails you've created, if a guest has to wander and look around for a place to put their coat, you've missed the first—and most important—opportunity to make them feel welcome.

Station two people by the door. When guests arrive, one person can usher them in while the other stays to greet others. This is the perfect time to give guests information:

Welcome! Would you like to put your purse in the hall closet? or Thanks for coming. The bar is open on the deck, just down the hall and to the right.

Tip

SNIP THAT STAMEN

The florist created gorgeous orchid arrangements for our office open house, but throughout the evening they left bright yellow pollen all over the carpet. During any floral consultation, ask about removing stamens to avoid staining carpets—and guests' clothing.

Try this!

LIVING STATUES STAND AND DELIVER

Living statues—or models who dress in costume and stand still for long periods of time—make fabulous conversation pieces. For the firm's open house, we had living statues of the woman on the scales of justice and the Statue of Liberty positioned in highly visible areas. A little costume rental and makeup creates silent entertainment that speaks volumes.

Pictured left to right: **Robert Feiger, a Lady Justice living statue, and Larry Friedman**

ENTERTAINMENT MAKES A BIG SPLASH

When Larry and I had an open house at our new home, I hired the beloved halftime dancers for the Dallas Mavericks—a large group of large men called the Mav ManiAACs—to dance in the pool. And they put on quite a show. Everyone was hysterical with laughter at something so out of character for an open house and people still mention it to me years later. Here are a few more ways to up the fun factor:

❋ Do a twist on the traditional caricature and bring in an artist to sketch guests' butts. You read that right: butts. It immediately gets everyone laughing and sets the tone for a fun event.

❋ Hire a musician who does more than one thing. For an open house at my son Brian's event space, I had a DJ who also played the guitar and violin. You get a lot of diverse music for one price.

❋ Cigar rollers

❋ A cappella groups—doo wop, barbershop quartets, choirs

❋ Nail artists

❋ Henna artists

❋ Chair massages/foot massages

PARTING GIFTS: TAKE IT TO THE BANK

I've done hundreds of different party favors over the years, but my favorite were the ceramic banks I bought and wrapped in cellophane. I put a note inside that said, "Thank you for coming and wishing us well Take this bank home, fill it up and give it to your favorite charity."

Favors send guests off with a smile, but they don't always have to be given out after the event. Have photos taken of guests, then frame and send them as thank-yous afterward to highlight your gratitude.

Here are some other favors I've loved:

- Hire an engraver to create personalized compacts for ladies and business card holders for men.

- Hire a photographer to stand at the front door and take headshots of each guest. Print them, cut out the faces, and put them on bobbleheads.

Sweeten the send-off: fill a table near the exit with different kinds of candy in beautiful glass jars so guests can load up little bags to go.

Guests love to watch rollers create fresh, handmade cigars and the band is a perfect place to add a party or business logo.

Red, red wine

A PAIN IN THE STAIN

Unless it's a seated dinner, I never serve red wine inside my home. There's always a spill, always a stain, and always a guest who feels terrible about it. Couches and carpets can be replaced, but guests spend the remainder of the event feeling embarrassed, so I avoid anything that distracts them from having a good time.

Serve red wine outside, then station people at the doors who offer to hold guests' drinks while they tour the house.

OH GOODIE!
From brochures to business cards and snacks to Silly Putty, gift bags are a great way to send guests home with more than a smile.

love and celebration

ENGAGEMENT PARTIES

WHEN

The timing of an engagement party depends on the length of the engagement. My daughter Heather's engagement was a year and a half long, so we held her party six months after she was engaged. My son Eric planned on a one-year engagement, so we held his party three months after the proposal. There's no rule, but make sure it feels like a separate event and not part of the wedding festivities.

WHERE

I prefer to host engagement parties at my home so they feel intimate, but I've also seen them done well at an event space or restaurant.

GUEST LIST

If you invite a guest to the engagement party, you also have to invite them to the wedding—so think through the list carefully.

ONE-BITE BEAUTIES

All-white desserts create delicious decor with a bridal look and feel.

Dating is all about dialogue: we share stories, ask questions, and talk about our families and friends. But after all the communication and conversation, it only takes five words to change two lives:

Will you marry me? *Yes!*

When anyone you love gets engaged, it's an exciting time—and hosting an engagement party is a wonderful way to surround the couple with love and celebration. Much like the engagement itself, a successful engagement party starts with a few simple words:

1. *Don't*
2. *Go*
3. *Overboard.*

Keep it simple. Keep it elegant. An engagement party should create excitement around a wedding, not be a mini version of one.

PRESENT MOMENT

The Gift Table

I never set aside a table for gifts when I'm having an event in my home, but I also don't want gifts cluttering up every table in the house. So I have greeters at the door take the gift and deliver it to a designated room.

The most important part of this transaction is making sure a card is attached to each gift to avoid having to figure out who brought what when it comes to thank-you time. Always keep tape near the door in case the card and gift aren't attached.

To Open or Not to Open?

Some brides want to open gifts during the party and some don't. Guests usually don't enjoy sitting for hours and watching someone else open gifts. But if it's what the bride wants, make sure you have people on hand to help put gifts back in the box, pick up trash, and keep the flow moving along.

The Thank-You Timeline

Guests should receive a thank-you note from the couple within thirty days of the engagement party.

ARRANGED MARRIAGE
Use tall floral arrangements to add height to buffet tables. Incorporate flowers with neutral scents so they don't compete with the food.

WHITE BITES

Host an engagement party open house–style and serve all white desserts and cocktails to keep with the wedding theme. It's easier and less expensive than doing dinner and allows for a casual event.

* Meringue kisses

* Traditional petit fours

* "Making whoopee" pies

* Petite snowball cupcakes

* White chocolate trifle shooters

* White chocolate–dipped shortbread cookie pops

* Mini bride and groom monogram sugar cookies

* Mini coconut cream pies with Italian meringue

Wedding White Cosmopolitan
vodka, white cranberry juice, and freshly squeezed lime

Wedding Cake Martini
vanilla vodka, white rum, coconut rum, pineapple juice, and a splash of grenadine. Rim the glass with crushed white candy

Sparkling White Sangria
white grapes, pineapple, and star fruit served in a white wine glass

White Wine Margarita
chardonnay, limeade, and orange juice served in a margarita glass rimmed with superfine white sugar

White Champagne Margarita
white tequila, triple sec, and sweetened lime juice topped with champagne and served in a flute

keep it casual & simple

The Friedman Factor:

START AT THE STREET

Setting the tone for any event begins long before guests walk through the door. For Heather's engagement party, I used a local production company to make a vinyl carpet printed with their names, picture, and words describing their relationship:

- California (their wedding destination)
- She said yes!
- Believe
- Faith
- It's the real thing.
- Serenity
- Bluffton (the groom's hometown)
- Love
- Indiana (where they met)
- Hope

There were also paw prints to symbolize Heather's career as a dog trainer. We had the carpet laid from the street to the front door and guests had a great time reading it as they walked toward the house. It also made for a cute picture of the couple.

For Eric's engagement party, I used the same production company to create a massive 12"x 12" framed color photo of him and his fiancée, Ilona, that we positioned on the front lawn. Believe me, no guest went to the wrong house looking for the party either night.

Another cool outdoor conversation starter is the Airstar, or giant helium-filled balloon. We used one for Heather's engagement party and it lit up the entire backyard. She went around telling everyone, "Look, my daddy bought me the moon!"

Tip

THE LAW ON IN-LAWS

It's often said that engagement parties are the first time two families come together, but I don't believe that's true. The families have usually met long before the couple is engaged. It's important to make the future in-laws feel welcome at an engagement party, but not to the point where you feel obligated to include them in the party planning. This follows one of my top entertaining rules: if you're paying, you get to decide what happens.

Try this!

HAVE FUN WITH FATE

When done right, having entertainment at an engagement party can highlight —instead of distract from—the couple.

For Eric's, I hired a magician who predicted their futures. He brought the couple in front of everyone and had them tell each other what they were looking forward to about their lives as husband and wife. Then he made lots of jokes about what really happens in marriage. It was a fun way to add new energy and give guests something to do besides eat, drink, and chitchat.

Entertainers are also a great way to handle toasts. If you want to avoid bogging down the energy of the party with endless toasts, have the entertainer give one to close up the show.

Here are some other magical ways to liven up the event:

❊ If the couple documents their engagement with a video, play it at the party.

❊ A video montage of pictures of the bride and groom from birth to present day is always a fun thing for guests to watch. Play it on repeat so guests can catch different parts throughout and not feel like they have to watch it all in one sitting.

❊ Separate the guests into groups and do a wine tasting. Try it blindfolded!

❊ Engage guests with a trivia game about the couple and have a grand prize for the winner.

❊ Host your own version of *The Newlywed Game*, starring the engaged couple, the bride's parents, and the groom's parents.

the lovely couple

make it beautiful, and personal

DESTINATION WEDDINGS

Create a cohesive feel at outdoor weddings by adding small bouquets to the end of each aisle.

Right before she turned the planning of her entire wedding over to me, my oldest daughter, Heather, said, "Mom, I don't care what you do—I know it's all going to be beautiful. But I have one thing to ask: I want to know everyone who attends my wedding."

Here's one of those wedding planning rules no one says out loud: *Destination weddings are the best way to make sure that everyone who attends has a real connection to the couple.* It's easy to get in the car and drive to a hotel; it's not as easy—or affordable—to set aside an entire weekend, arrange accommodations, and get on a plane.

When everyone's on vacation, the entire event—from rehearsal dinner to ceremony—feels relaxed. Family members reconnect. Strangers become friends. The bride and groom have real conversations with guests throughout the weekend instead of trying to thank everyone at the reception. And best of all, a destination wedding feels substantial—an event worthy of all the effort and expense that went into it.

Don't try to compete with the sand and sea: Choose simple statement florals like white roses, lilies, and lush green foliage that complement the surroundings.

SET THE TONE IN STYLE

INVITATION ONLY

Invitations are so much more than pretty paper and envelopes—they set the tone for the entire event. Whether the style is casual or formal, playful or traditional, guests assume the occasion will follow suit.

Destination wedding invitations start with a save-the-date, followed by an invitation a few months later. To create a cohesive feel, use the wedding color scheme or theme for all correspondence.

THE TIMELINE

I'm a big believer in getting invitations out early and asking for RSVPs early as well, especially if it's a seated dinner.

❊ For an in-town wedding, the save-the-date isn't necessary. Send the invite six to eight weeks prior to the event and ask guests to RSVP one month before the event.

❊ For a destination wedding, send the save-the-date as soon as possible to give people time to make plans and get good travel rates. Send the invite four to six months in advance and ask guests to RSVP two months before the event.

❊ Thank-you notes—the couple's responsibility—should hit mailboxes no more than two months after the wedding.

On the RSVP date, I start calling, texting, or emailing people who haven't responded. People forget, get busy, or don't understand the purpose of an RSVP. The goal isn't to berate a guest for not responding, but to remind them how excited you are about the event and that you need to know who's coming so you can move forward with food and beverage, seating, and other details.

For my daughter's destination wedding in Santa Monica, the invitation was designed to match the sea. I had silk pouches made to act as the envelope and tied the theme together with a small shell.

SHELL GAME
Invite nature to beach weddings by working oyster pearl crystals and blush-colored shells into arrangements with coral and white flowers.

ATTENTION TO DETAIL

TAG, YOU'RE IT!

For Heather's save-the-date, I had luggage tags made with the name and address of each guest. This accomplished a dual mission: it got everyone excited about the wedding and, when guests arrived at the hotel, employees immediately knew they were there for our event.

GOOD TIMES, BAD NEWS

At any event, as in life, something always goes wrong. If you have to deliver bad news to a guest, be honest. Sugarcoating or lying only makes things worse.

For Heather's wedding, I picked out specific hotel rooms for each guest. When I went to visit my parents, they were in the wrong room. I felt terrible having to ask another guest to change rooms, but I explained the situation, apologized for the inconvenience, and let them know I'd do everything in my power to make the transition an easy one. If you are gracious, people will usually respond that way as well.

KEEP IT REAL

The night before the wedding, Heather decided to have an energy drink at midnight. It threw her whole body off and she was sick all night, all morning, and still shaky five minutes before she walked down the aisle.

While you want the bride and groom to have the time of their lives, it's important to remind them not to do anything they wouldn't normally do in the days leading up to the wedding.

Tip

Include an RSVP card or email address with the save-the-date to get a good idea of your numbers early. You may be able to invite more people than you think.

WEATHER OR NOT

Chilly beach evenings call for cashmere shawls. Stack them on a table near the entrance with a note that lets guests know they're theirs to keep.

THE OUTDOOR "I DO"

No matter where you live, the number one concern when planning an outdoor wedding is always the weather. Having a Plan B is essential. When vetting venues, look for a place that has indoor and outdoor options. You may have to pay more to reserve a ballroom you won't use, but it's better than letting Mother Nature decide whether the wedding is a success or not.

JUDGING THE JUDGE

Whether it's a rabbi, priest, judge, preacher, or someone with an online minister's certificate, it's up to the couple to choose an officiant for their ceremony. If someone they know and trust isn't available, they should interview others in person and attend their services a few times until they find someone who feels right.

That said, a bad officiant can make or break a ceremony. While it's the couple's call, I suggest having a few conversations with their choice as well—just to add another layer of insurance that all goes smoothly.

THE WEDDING PLANNER: NECESSITY OR LUXURY?

If it's a big wedding and the budget allows for it, I highly suggest having a wedding planner. Because no matter how much work you do on the front end, you will eventually have to take your seat. At that point, it's time to be present and enjoy yourself while a wedding planner takes care of the bride, coordinates everyone getting down the aisle, and manages all the details of the reception—seating, flowers, place cards, etc.—while you soak in the moments you've worked so hard to create.

THE HOT SEATS

When I go to a sit-down affair, I prefer to have an assigned seat. I like knowing I have a place to land instead of having to hunt down a table. When I give a party, I extend that same courtesy to guests. I don't want them to think about anything but having a good time.

Putting the right people at the right tables is a major factor in guest satisfaction and, much like a puzzle, takes a lot of trial and error before it all fits perfectly. Years ago my mother taught me a trick that has never failed me. And all you need is a pen and a stack of index cards.

Most event spaces will have a schematic of the room and number of tables—if not, draw your own. But don't write names on the tables—this is a common mistake and will make the whole thing take twice as long. Write each couple's name on an index card. Put five cards on each table (totaling ten people) and start moving them around, pairing up friends, family, and business acquaintances.

WEDDING CAKES:
DECOR OR DELICIOUS?

Keep the celebration going by hiring a band or singers to guide guests from the ceremony to the reception.

Marriage is a long, wonderful road. Start the ride in style by sending the couple off in a carriage or cool old car.

CAKE: THE STYROFOAM SECRET

Everyone loves a big, beautiful cake but there's a not-so-sweet side to it: wedding cakes often look better than they taste.

For Heather's wedding, I hired a well-known pastry chef in New York City to create the cake and ship it layer by layer to Southern California. It was gorgeous but tasted terrible. If I had to do it all over again, I'd have the chef create a delicious bottom layer and decorate Styrofoam for the rest.

That's right: Styrofoam.

Any other way is too expensive and wasteful. I've also seen it done where the entire cake is Styrofoam except for a small section that the couple cuts, then the pastry chef makes a wedding sheet cake to

match. It's so much fresher and makes it much quicker to cut in the kitchen and serve. Terrible wedding cake can literally leave a bad taste in guests' mouths.

MORE FOOD FOR THOUGHT

If there are gaps between the wedding and reception, fill in with a cocktail hour. Guests don't mind waiting for wedding party photos or the venue to set up as long as they have a drink, a snack, and some-where to sit.

Heather's wedding was at sundown in the summer, meaning dinner would be later in the evening. Before the ceremony, we did a cocktail hour with seafood and drinks so guests wouldn't be starving as soon as they got to the reception.

SLICE OF HEAVEN
A true showstopper wedding cake should look good and taste good. Never settle for one without the other.

LOVE AT FIRST BITE

You don't need a culinary degree to know that cooking for two is different than cooking for two hundred. So while multiple menu tastings are crucial, it's just as important to make sure the chef is there with the food.

Ask if the food will taste and look the same at the event as it does the day of your tasting. Discuss special requests like vegan, vegetarian, nut-, dairy-, or gluten-free meals for guests. Communicate your needs so they know exactly what it'll take to make you and your guests happy.

Not all wedding dinners have to be seated affairs. Chart a different course by doing food stations or an elegant buffet. If you have more than 150 people, create two buffet lines—one on each end—to cut down on guests having to wait too long.

WEDDING MENU INSPIRATION

Salad

Golden beets with blue cheese and Belgian endive

Appetizer

Seared sea scallops with oven-dried tomatoes or Wagyu beef carpaccio

Intermezzo

Sweet summer sorbet

Main course

Mediterranean sea bass, baby octopus, jumbo prawns, and little neck clams with braised fennel

or

Filet with truffle sauce, truffle whipped potatoes, and white asparagus

Dessert

Wedding and groom's cake

Cheese course

Gorgonzola dolce with figs, mostarda, and walnuts

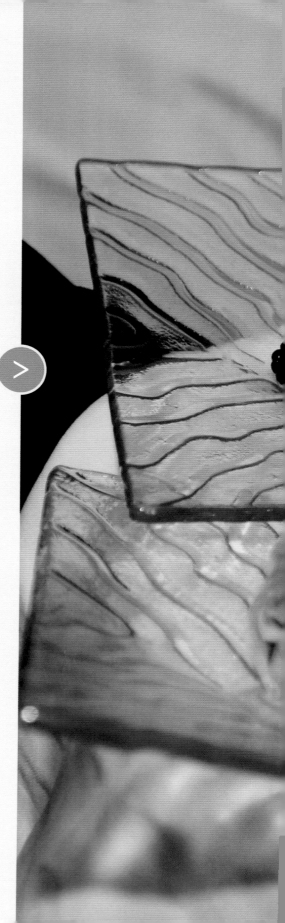

The Friedman Factor:

BEAUTY AND THE BEACH

Heather's destination wedding was in Southern California and the majority of the guests were from Dallas. Instead of sending guests scrambling for a salon, I decided to create one for them.

After three rooms were cleared of beds and furniture, we installed salon chairs and mirrors and brought in hairstylists and makeup artists. Guests made appointments in advance and received a confirmation card for the complimentary service at check-in.

Here are a few other ways to spoil guests silly:

⁜ Go big on the welcome gift: we set up a desk in the lobby and staffed it with someone to greet each wedding guest. Everyone got a beautiful tote bag with a beach towel and itinerary for the weekend.

⁜ Outdoor wedding at sunset? Set a big basket of cashmere wraps by the entrance to keep the ladies warm.

⁜ At the reception, have monogrammed coasters made for each guest. They double as a table assignment and wedding favor.

FOND FAREWELL

 Send the couple off in style. Heather got married over the Fourth of July, so we said goodbye with sparklers. Here are more ways to create that picture-perfect moment:

⁜ Balloons in wedding colors

⁜ Biodegradable confetti

⁜ Biodegradable Chinese lanterns

⁜ Rose petals

⁜ Bubbles

⁜ Ribbon wands

⁜ Dried lavender

⁜ Mini beach balls

a big party for a big personality

Janelle and Larry Friedman

want to party with you at

THE
S T A R C K
CLUB

Saturday, June 11, 2011

8:00 p.m.

Night Club Attire

ONE NIGHT ONLY

chapter 4

Take guests back in time with a party that celebrates the best of their younger years.

"One Night Only" was code for a milestone birthday for my husband, Larry. He is a big personality who deserved a celebration to match, but he didn't want to be the center of attention. So I changed the name and invited all the people who have touched his life throughout the years.

Even by Texas standards, One Night Only was the party to end all parties. Of all the events I've planned, it's the one that left the most profound effect on guests—so much so that they still mention it to me years later.

What I wouldn't give to live that night over again.

GET A CLUE
Who says an invitation has to give out every detail of the party? Use pictures to give hints at what you have planned and curiosity will keep the RSVPs rolling in.

ABOVE IT ALL
Think vertically: multilevel event spaces give guests a new perspective from each floor.

RECREATING A SPACE

In the '70s and '80s, Dallas's version of Studio 54 was a place called the Starck Club. From the music to celebrities and even the co-ed bathrooms— it was all like being on a different and very decadent planet.

It had long since closed down on the day I happened to drive by, but seeing the building brought back such good memories. And then it hit me: I'd recreate the Starck Club for Larry's party.

You can recreate anything as long as you lock in on the look and feel. An Italian restaurant can become the trattoria you frequented during your honeymoon with a few simple touches.

VETTING THE VENUE

Use crystals to create soft drapes from the ceiling and shroud columns with sparkle.

Chair covers are an easy way to turn boring chairs into pretty perches for guests.

Create different sections of the space that carry the overall theme. At One Night Only, some spaces seemed private, like VIP areas, where others were meant for guests to see and be seen.

When scoping out any venue, always go with your gut. When something doesn't feel right, my go-to line is "I'm not feeling it." If it feels right, ask these questions to make sure all the bases are covered:

* Is there a kitchen? If the answer is yes, is there adequate space for my catering needs? If not, is there room outside to tent and set up a satellite kitchen?

* What's the parking situation? Do I need a valet?

* Will I have to get special permits to close off streets?

* How early can we start the installation of lighting, sound, and decor? (One Night Only took eight days.)

* Can I have a three-day window to take everything down after the event?

* Are there backup generators?

* Can existing furnishings be removed or repositioned?

* What role will the venue play in the event? Do they have a service staff, cleaning and maintenance on-site during the party, plumbers, electricians, etc.?

* Are they willing to sign a confidentiality agreement if necessary?

* Are there any events taking place nearby on the same date that could affect traffic?

* Is the venue willing to sign a release so I can use their brand on invitations or take photos on the property?

* Can I bring my own branded items that the venue would normally provide (i.e., napkins for the bar, towels for the bathroom)?

* Can I use my own vendors for food, bar, flowers, etc.?

* Will their staff wear specific uniforms or costumes?

* Will their staff attend training for specific instructions about the event?

* Are there any additional rooms or offices I can use as green rooms, tech rooms for storage, or areas for the talent to have meals before the events?

* Will there be any changes to the venue prior to the event?

* Can we do a site inspection with the city's special events office and fire marshal before signing?

AIM FOR THE STARS

STAR FACTOR

Wonder what it would be like to have a celebrity sing at your party? It's easier than you think. Some quick Internet research can determine what agency represents the artist and a quick call will let you know their availability and cost.

Agencies are a fantastic source for performers of all kinds. Just tell them what you're looking for and they can suggest people in that field.

DON'T MISS A MINUTE

When you go to the effort of planning multiple experiences for guests, make sure they know about them. Everyone at One Night Only received a card when they arrived detailing food and entertainment in all areas of the venue, from foot massages in the women's bathrooms to the timing of various entertainment and food service.

TAKE THE CAKE

A once-in-a-lifetime party demands a once-in-a-lifetime cake. Do something daring and different. For another of Larry's milestone birthdays, I had a massive cake made with a cake version of myself coming out of the top of it holding another cake. The pastry chef even matched the color of the dress I wore that night. It was the ultimate edible conversation piece.

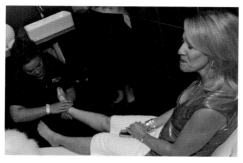

Ladies love to kick off their high heels for free foot massages in the bathroom.

My friends still tease me about this oversized cake I had made to look like me popping out of a cake with another cake in my hand.

ICE, ICE, BABY!
Guests went wild for Vanilla Ice, who performed a personal concert at One Night Only. Nothing creates a big buzz like a legendary entertainer.

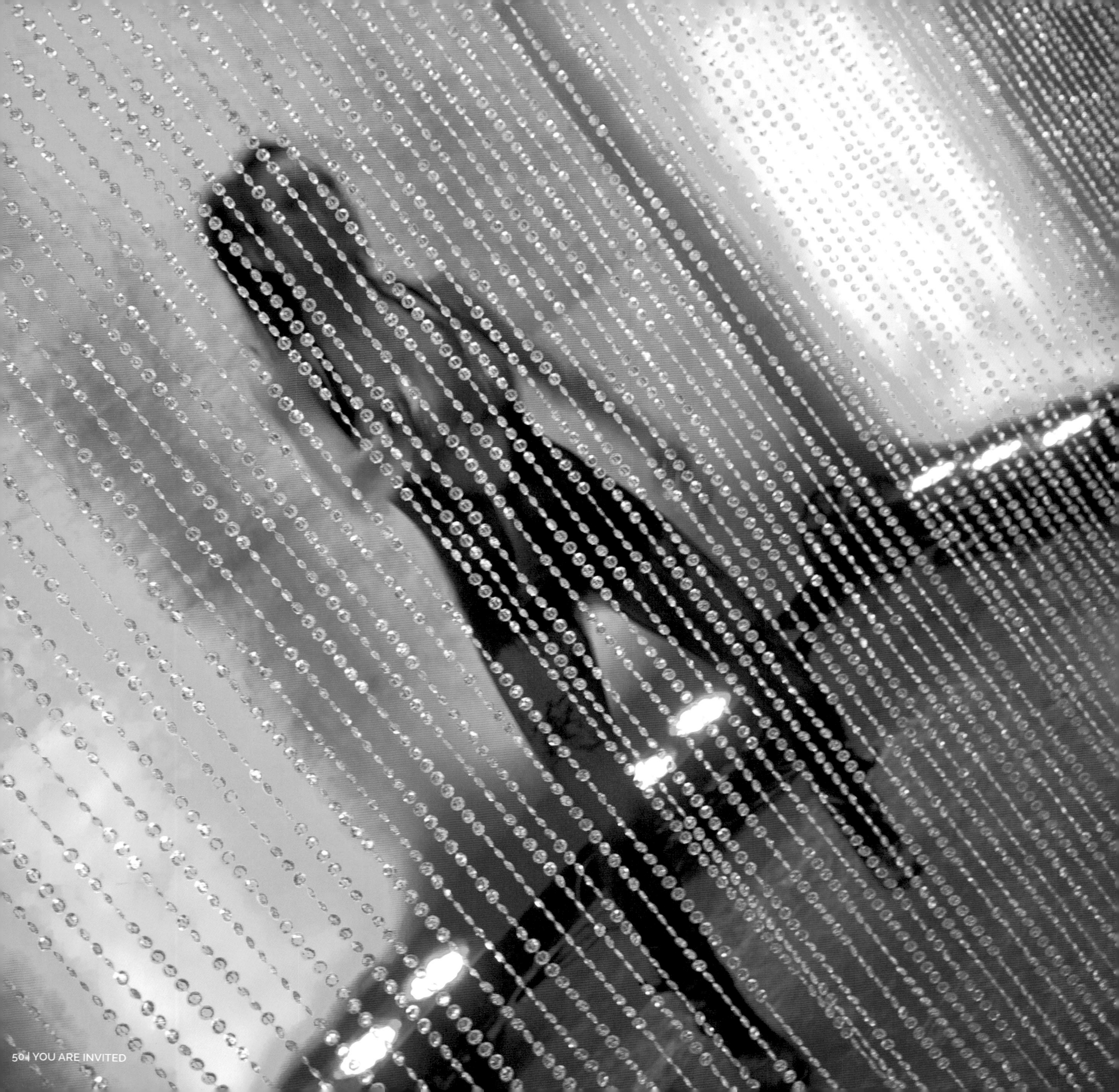

KEEP THE ENERGY ALIVE

As the party wore on, models with dim sum carts danced their way through the crowd, serving up sushi and hot hand towels.

Do something completely different: Hire aerial artists to perform on the side of the building and wow guests from the walkway.

HIRE LEARNING

It's easy to get fixated on food, drinks, and decor when you're throwing a big bash, but a big part of recreating the Starck Club was hiring people to play the part. Go-go dancers and drag queens paraded around inside while acrobats did aerial tricks on the scaffolding out front.

Whether the theme is sock hop or *Star Wars*, performers are living, breathing, moving ambience who can interact with guests and keep the energy alive.

WOO WITH CLUES

To build excitement around the party, I used a bound book of clues about the theme and performers as the invitation. Every picture gave a little hint about the evening and it generated lots of talk about the party. Months in advance, guests felt like I was planning a surprise just for them. This might have something to do with the fact that we had a 1,000-person guest list and not many RSVP'd no.

OH SHOOT!

When guests arrived at One Night Only, they walked through a little booth, pressed a button and snapped a photo of themselves. At the end of the night, everyone went home with a flash drive with all the pictures of the party. It was a digital photo album at their fingertips.

The Friedman Factor:

URGE TO SPLURGE

Having custom clothing made—or giving the guest of
honor a special accessory—adds an extra layer of love
to their experience.

Despite Larry's hesitation to be the center of attention,
he had no choice once he put on the jacket he'd had
custom-made for the event. I was dressed to the nines
and no one even looked my way.

A MEAL TO REMEMBER

Passed appetizers

❋ Butternut squash spoon bread

❋ Taquito with mango and caramelized onions

❋ Spicy tuna tartar in sesame cone

❋ Trio of chilled soup shooters: classic vichyssoise, heirloom tomato gazpacho, English pea

Small plates

❋ Sea scallops over mascarpone polenta and asparagus tips amandine

❋ Pheasant breast tenders with honey mustard and Texas field pea salad

❋ Swedish meatballs with whipped potatoes and tomato gravy

Late-night dim sum

❋ Chicken pot stickers

❋ Shrimp shumai

make a difference

CHARITY EVENTS

chapter 5

If the favor is small, use it as part of the place setting.

I had a life-changing moment many years ago at lunch with Larry and Ann and Nate Levine, friends who are very involved in local philanthropy. They asked about our kids. They asked about the law firm. And after we filled them in on all the details of our busy lives, they asked a very interesting question: "What are you doing for your community?"

It's been ages, but I can still remember exactly how I felt as their words sunk in. I sat there stunned, with nothing to say. And it hit me: I was missing out on the opportunity to help others.

After that night, I wasted no time getting involved. And whether I spend a few hours serving soup to the homeless or an entire year coordinating a gala filled with food, speeches, and celebrity entertainment, the purpose is always the same: make a difference in someone's life. It always feels good to do good.

HUE'S WHO
Something as simple as alternating tablecloths and acrylic chairs makes a hotel ballroom feel warm and personal.

SEE THE LIGHT
Creative lighting is the key to transforming a hotel ballroom into a space full of intentional ambiance. Flattering levels of light and interesting designs on the walls add much-needed personality and dimension.

COMING TOGETHER FOR A CAUSE

BY THE NUMBERS

When Children's Health, one of the nation's leading pediatric healthcare systems, asked Larry and me to chair their one hundredth anniversary party—the Celebration of Our Century—I was very touched. My family and everyone I know have been affected in some way by their organization and I made it my mission not to let them down.

Chairing a benefit is much different than hosting a personal party. When I host a party, I'm in charge and make all the decisions. But chairing a benefit means working for some-one else with their own approval process. It's harder—and often more stressful—but always worth it.

Before you agree to host or help plan a benefit, make sure you understand all the goals and feel confident they're attainable. This goes for the financial goals as well. It's important to be very careful when you're spending someone else's money. Ask about the budget for expenses and how much money needs to be raised, then create your own budget focused on the goal.

Tip

One of the biggest expenses of any large party is audiovisual. This includes everything from lighting and speakers to screens for entertainment and presentations. When estimating expenses, start there and work your way down the list.

SET THE STAGE
Large galas have hundreds of moving parts and lots of cooks in the kitchen. The secret to a successful event is never losing sight of the people for whom you're raising money. If you channel that passion into every detail of the event, guests will feel it as well.

PUNCH UP THE PERSONALITY

The Pointer Sisters perform on stage at the Children's Health benefit.

An easy way to cut costs and make more money for the charity involves asking vendors to donate their services or offer a reduced rate. I've been very successful in getting choirs, musicians, stationers, and others to donate their time or services—especially if it's someone I use regularly. It makes their business look good to be included on a contributor's list and decreases the amount of money you have to spend on behalf of the charity. Everyone wins.

MORE THAN THE MONEY

A charity event has a higher purpose than a party—one that should always take center stage. For the Children's Health benefit, all the entertainment revolved around the children until the Pointer Sisters and Jennifer Hudson took the stage after dinner.

The hospital recommended two children who'd benefited from their services and we used them in a videotaped skit about getting dressed for the ball. We also brought in one hundred kids from Dallas Children's Theater to do a ceremony with red balloons. It was adorable and a nice reminder of the people who really benefit from everyone's contributions.

PAPER CHASE

I love a statement invitation for personal parties, but charity invites are best kept simple for cost conservation. Yours may share space in recipients' mailboxes with a stack of others, but it's not about standing out—it's about helping others. If your cause speaks to people, they'll attend.

CRYSTAL CLEAR
Something as simple as a few strands of crystals hung as a backdrop adds a layer of elegance and visual interest to an otherwise unremarkable area.

focus on the details

EVERY GREAT PARTY STARTS WITH A NOTEBOOK, A LIST AND A PLAN

Bubbles anyone? Section off a small area for a Champagne bar so guests can toast, refill, and repeat.

Color-coordinated tablecloths and chargers bring this ballroom to life.

RED ALERT
Use colored glassware to add a pop of color to the table.

TABLE TALK

With large spaces and built-in food and beverage, hotel ballrooms offer lots of bang for the buck. The key to making your event look different than all the others hosted in that space lies in the small details.

* Switch out the sea of round tables and rent ones in various shapes—serpentine, oblong, square, oval, etc.—to give the room a unique feel.

* Something as simple as a colored charger can make such a visual difference on the tabletop. We did everything in red for the Children's Health benefit: red champagne glasses, square and triangular dishware, and cones for dessert service.

* Ditch the hotel linens: pick out pretty tablecloths and napkins to make each table pop.

THE PAPER TRAIL

If you don't get everything in writing, it will come back and kick you in the butt. Never be afraid to ask for contracts with any vendor, big or small, friend, stranger, or Grammy-winning performer. For every event I plan, I have a notebook with a list of every vendor—lighting, caterers, rentals, etc.—and their contact information. And right behind that list goes the contracts for each.

When something goes wrong—and something always goes wrong—I don't have to go home and flip through endless files. I can go straight to my contract and settle things on the spot.

FEED THE NEED

Charity events usually have speeches, so I make sure guests have something to eat while the talking takes place. For a lunch I'll do dips, vegetables, hummus, and olives. For dinner, I'll have a shareable appetizer like crab cakes set between every two people. That way guests can concentrate and enjoy instead of starving and waiting impatiently for the program to be over.

After the speeches, it's time for food service. At lunch I'll have a salad sampler or light meal served family style. Dinner needs to be more substantial, like steak or fish. As with any event, doing multiple tastings is extremely important to make sure you don't wind up with the proverbial rubber chicken dinner.

Appetizer Shared by Two

* Crab Cakes with Tomato Jam and Barbecue Shrimp
* Grilled Sriracha Peppers
* Composed Salad
* Caesar Salad
* Edamame Salad
* Herbed Baby Bibb

Entrée Trio

* Miso Cod with Shishito Peppers
* Five Spiced Beef with Ginger Scallion Sauce
* Lamb Shank

Dessert A Quartet of Sweets:

* Five-Spiced Chocolate Cake, Vanilla Cream
* Blueberry Panna Cotta, Ginger Cream
* Classic Lemon Curd, Yuzu Cream
* Chocolate-Sesame Cheesecake Lollipop

Time Tip

One of my biggest pet peeves is when I walk into an event and dessert is already on the table. It speaks to the freshness of the food and the level of service the waitstaff is willing to give. Dessert and coffee service should always follow dinner.

EYES ON THE PRIZE

DEALING WITH DRAMA

Chairing events and serving on committees can be a wonderful bonding experience. Over the years I've turned many acquaintances into friends during the process.

But there are always stresses and frustrations. I've been on many committees where it took ten members all night to decide on a napkin color. I've learned to pick my battles: if napkin color is your battle, fight it. If not, go with the flow and focus on the things that are more important to you.

I don't like drama, but it's inevitable. When it shows up, remember that you represent your community and family. Act in a way you can be proud of later when the heat dies down.

Drama can also be external. At one benefit I helped host, we had a speaker— a notable person to whom we'd paid thousands of dollars—who refused to dine with the guests. Though we'd agreed in advance that she would dine with attendees—and set guest expectations that they'd have a meal with her—she decided to walk in, speak, and leave. Instead of covering it up or sugarcoating it, we explained to guests that she would not be joining them for lunch. Honesty is always the best policy.

BLACK TIE AND BEYOND

Dress codes can be hard to decipher. Use this primer to make sure your outfit matches the occasion:

* **Black tie:** Tuxedos (not suits) for men; cocktail dress or long gown for women,

* **Casual dress:** Nice jeans or pants for men and women, with regional exceptions. If it's a beachy or tropical location, shorts or sundresses are OK. In Dallas, casual dress means dressy casual: no jeans for women and nice jeans and a dress shirt for men—maybe even a sport coat.

* **Cocktail:** Suit and tie for men; cocktail dress for women.

* **Dinner party:** Sport coats for men unless the invite says casual; dinner dress or nice pants and top for women.

* **Formal:** Traditionally means a tuxedo for men and long gown for women, with some exceptions. If the invite says black tie optional, it can be suit and tie or tux for men and cocktail dress for women.

STRIKE A CHORD
Devote a big portion of your budget to hiring notable acts, like Starlight Orchestras, to give guests a private concert they'll never forget.

food makes fast friends

DINNER PARTIES

chapter 6

Guests are always more open to trying new things at a dinner party. Serve something exotic like uni, the edible part of a sea urchin.

For entertaining junkies like me, having a dinner party is a great way to get your fix between big events.

They don't require a reason. Maybe you want to get together with friends. Maybe you want to introduce people to each other. Maybe you bought a stack of plates made from fallen palm leaves (oh yes, these things exist!) and want to see them in action. Make some calls and make it happen.

They're just so wonderfully intimate. Instead of chatting over cocktails or yelling over the entertainment at a large event, dinner parties are designed for real conversations and connections. It never fails to amaze me how quickly acquaintances become friends over fantastic food and a great bottle of wine.

FEAST YOUR EYES
No Asian-themed place settings? No problem. Bento boxes make for colorful and creative presentations.

FASHION PLATES
Even more than the food, place settings set the tone for every dinner party and the mood for the meal. Add layer and dimension by mixing crystal and china, colors and textures, hardware (like candlesticks) with soft florals.

DESPITE THEIR NAME, DINNER PARTIES AREN'T SOLELY FOCUSED ON FOOD

BE MY GUEST

You can serve fresh lobster tails or frozen French fries—if your guests aren't able to hold a conversation, they'll just want to eat and leave.

Start with the right number of people: it depends on the size of your table, but I keep my guest list to sixteen people—couples, singles, or a mix of both.

For the guest list, think about common ground like jobs or occupations, neighborhoods or parts of town, religions or churches, kids or schools, or even people who have similar personalities or goals.

Once you've nailed that down, it's time for the seating chart—I always do one, unless it's close friends or family. The goal is for guests to have enough similarities to keep conversations going and enough differences to keep things interesting.

MAKE THE CALL

As much as I love to get my hands on a stack of envelopes and stamps, dinner parties don't require an invitation. Just pick up the phone, let guests know the date and time and that you'd love to have them. If you ask far in advance, follow up the week before with a text or email reminder.

Tip

When making out the guest list, add two alternate couples who will work well with the group. That way, if someone can't attend or has to cancel at the last minute, you have a backup in place.

TAKE YOUR SEAT

After you set the table, sit down in every seat and make sure you can see every other chair clearly. Keeping the tablescape low ensures that guests won't have to compete with flowers and other decor to interact with each other.

keep things interesting

CHEW ON THIS

I love to have a specialty chef—someone everyone knows—do the food. It adds another layer of entertainment and excitement to have the chef come out and introduce each course along with a sommelier who pairs the wines.

If I have specific ideas, I'll share them and we'll go back and forth on the menu a few times until it's perfect.

TRY THIS AT HOME

- ❊ Serve breakfast for dinner: bacon, eggs, and biscuits or a scrambled egg taco bar

- ❊ Do a custom pizza party—offer all kinds of toppings and crusts, including gluten- and dairy-free

- ❊ Do an all-Asian theme and serve it family style with monogrammed chopsticks

Here's some menu inspiration for an Eastern feast:

Tuna Sashimi, Family Style
White ponzu, chili oil, crisp ginger

Shrimp and Kimchi Pancakes for Two
Bonito flakes, dashi soy sauce

Miso-Glazed Cod Fish
Chinese long beans, pickled ramps, radish

Soft Shell Crab
Fresh herb salad, avocado, sweet chili vinaigrette

Seared Scallops and Soba Noodles
Peanuts, ginger, cilantro

Char Siu Beef Short Ribs
Bok choy

Dessert for Two: Banana Haru-Maki
Tofu mousse, braised raspberries, goma ice cream plus shared plates of chocolate chip cookies, key lime pie, peanut butter bar

Green tea and coffee

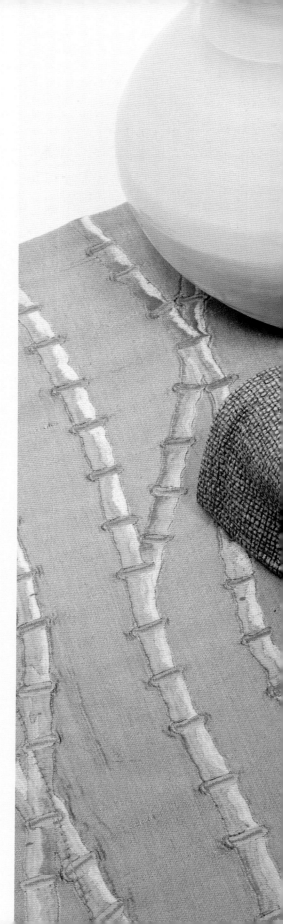

The Friedman Factor:

CHINA TOWN

Everyone collects something. Whether it's impressionist art or souvenir shot glasses, each piece tells a special story. Whenever Larry and I travel, we bring back place settings and serving pieces. He loves it when I set a beautiful table and enjoys picking out interesting pieces wherever we go.

We brought back a centerpiece from Israel and wine and champagne glasses from a china store in Canada that was an entire block long. On a trip to Capri, I found a six-foot-long series of serving dishes shaped like a fish—head, fins, tail. The shipping wound up costing more than the piece, but I could not leave without it. When I pull that thing out for dinner parties, everyone goes wild.

In our former home, where we raised kids for twenty-two years, my china and crystal were all over the house—under beds, in closets and cabinets. I barely knew where every piece was. When we built our current home, I added in plans for a room to display all our finds—nothing but wall-to-wall china in glass cases.

But it's not a museum. I use every single piece I have. One of the many things Larry has taught me is that material things are just that. Better to use it, enjoy it, and break it than never use it at all.

Any chef will tell you that cooking is about creating layers of flavor. Dressing the tabletop does the exact same thing. Start with a color and style and build from there, creating visual interest by pairing simple and ornate elements. Whether it's crystal stemware or jelly glasses, gold-plated chargers or mix-and-match vintage dishes, the key to a striking tabletop is remembering that everyone eats with their eyes first. *Make it mouthwatering.*

Set the Stage

FROM LEFT TO RIGHT, TOP TO BOTTOM:

Colorful placemats are an easy way to add a pop of color behind neutral china. For a springtime dinner, I chose a bright green placemat to accent the white plate and charger, then accessorized the table with green glassware and votives.

Try a wooden placemat with floral china for a light, natural look. For this dinner, I served Mediterranean spread with toast points as an appetizer and set a gold box at each place setting with the spread inside.

These rose dishes, by Red Pomegranate, jump right off the table. I paired them with Battenberg lace placemats and sterling flatware for a look that's both sexy and sweet.

Think beyond the plate. Here I used heavy crystal geode votives to complement the powerful color combination of teal and black. I softened the look with a white demitasse, from which I served consommé celestine.

This red charger makes a strong statement against the Versace by Rosenthal yellow plate and cup. I paired it with silver goblets from Israel, which insulate cold water. I never serve ice because it clinks and makes too much noise during conversation.

For a sophisticated Asian look, I had tea green placemats made with a bamboo pattern and offset the gold and black plates with jade sake cups. For an extra helping of elegance, I placed an orchid in the center of each curved appetizer plate.

Casual meets masculine in this look, with wooden and horn-handled flatware, gold-rimmed china, and a charger accented with laurel leaves. I used the sake cup as a shot glass for aquavit, a spicy spirit made in Scandinavia since the fifteenth century.

The right flatware can take a place setting from traditional to ultramodern in seconds. The mirrored placemat and platinum china add to the dressed-up look.

SET THE TABLE FOR A GORGEOUS EVENING

TABLETOP TOUCHES

Flowers and candles add depth and dimension to the table, but make sure they're high or low so they don't block the field of vision between guests. No matter how pretty those petals are, function should always trump form.

Guests expect plates and utensils, but are always surprised to find a personal piece on the table just for them. I've had photos taken of every couple when they arrive, then I print, frame, and place them by their seats. I've also had stemware and napkins monogrammed with each guest's initials. Details like that make guests feel special. They aren't hard—they aren't even expensive—they just take a little extra time.

THE HOME STRETCH

I've learned the hard way to expect the unexpected when entertaining at home. Years ago, when I gave a Mediterranean-themed party, the chef got into a fight with Mary, my housekeeper of twenty-seven years, who's very protective of us and our house. He took the food, left, and said he wasn't coming back.

This was one hour before the party.

I had to call, make nice, and beg him to come back. He eventually relented and it all went off without another hitch, but for a few moments there I thought I might have to start scrambling eggs.

throw a party for yourself

HAPPY BIRTHDAY TO ME

chapter 7

Guests scooped their favorite flavors of candy at one of the many "shops."

I've never understood why it's taboo to throw a party for your own birthday—it's the perfect time to celebrate all the people who make your world wonderful.

I've planned hundreds of parties over the years, always making sure to include everything the guest of honor loves most. Well, I love shopping and I love my friends. And as my fiftieth birthday drew near, I built a party around both.

What do you love? Who do you love? Bring them together and make some memories before there are more candles than cake.

GREEN WITH ENVY
Start with your favorite color and let it dictate the look and feel of everything from furniture to flowers.

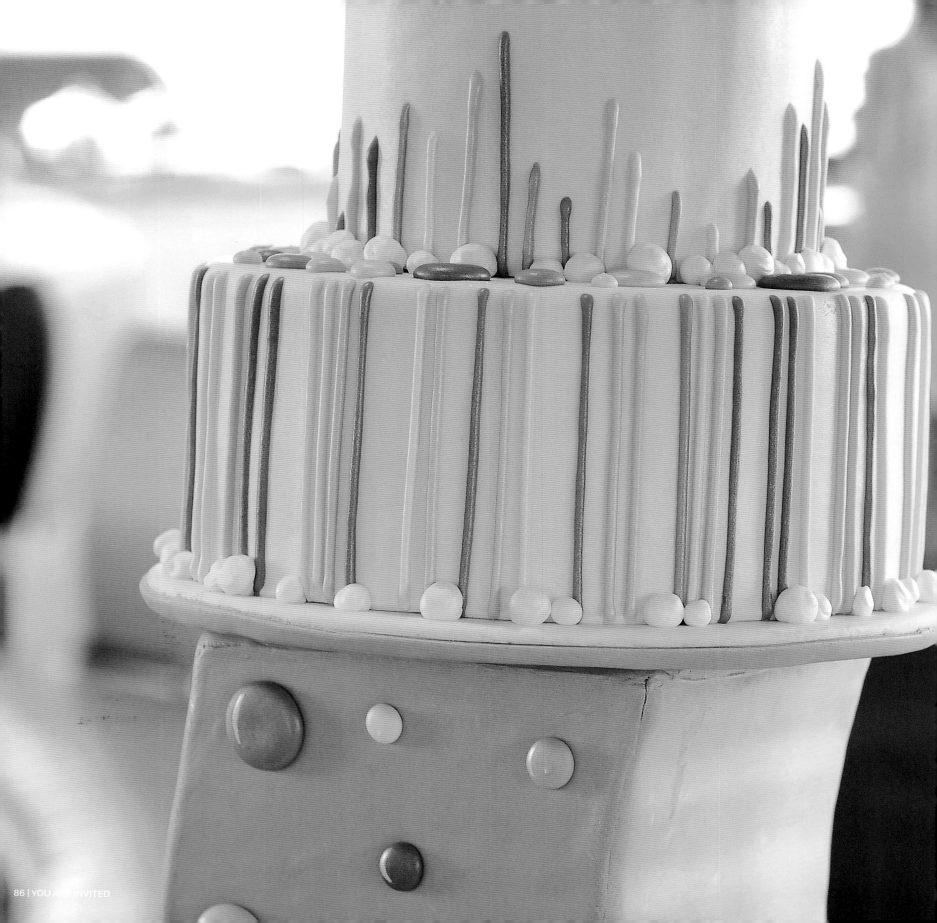

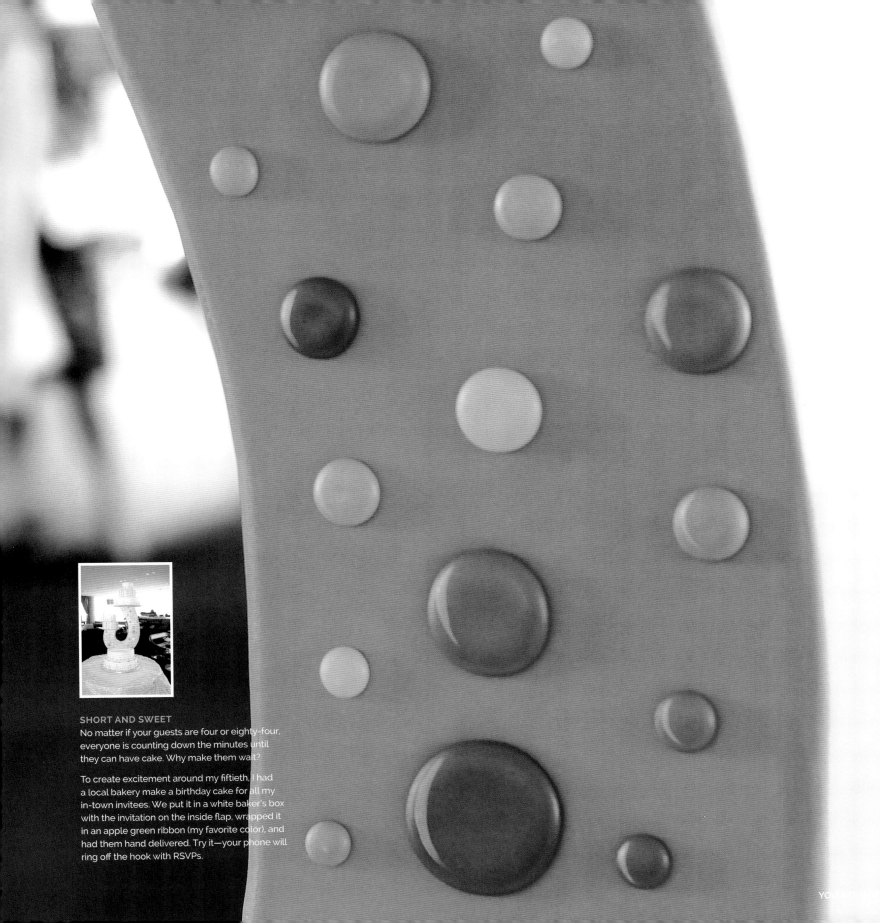

SHORT AND SWEET

No matter if your guests are four or eighty-four, everyone is counting down the minutes until they can have cake. Why make them wait?

To create excitement around my fiftieth, I had a local bakery make a birthday cake for all my in-town invitees. We put it in a white baker's box with the invitation on the inside flap, wrapped it in an apple green ribbon (my favorite color), and had them hand delivered. Try it—your phone will ring off the hook with RSVPs.

SET UP SHOP

Tip

BRAND TOGETHER

Some parties have a theme, color scheme, or logo. This one had all three. Instead of "Janelle's birthday," I called it the JLove party and had a logo created to personalize many of the gifts and other party favors, right down to the swizzle sticks.

SHOP TALK

As a wife and mother of six children, I've spent a lot of my life taking care of others. I didn't want a party fully focused on me; I wanted to use it as a way to give back to all the women who'd touched my life over the years. The goal was to fill our time together with drinks, food, fun, and gifts. And the shopping spree party was born.

Nail down the guest list first, then make a list of little gifts you love—artisan crafts, edible treats, fun trinkets, and more. Purchase them, then find a space where you can set up tables that will act as separate "shops." When each guest arrives, hand them a bag and have them shop their way around the room, taking whatever they want.

One of my favorite gifts was a coloring book I had created of my life story. Here are a few more things that found their way into guests' totes:

* Tea and biscotti in a mug
* Soaps
* Dolls with customizable dresses
* Makeup mirrors
* Lip gloss
* Notepads
* A disc of my favorite songs
* I also had a flower "shop" where guests could choose their favorites and have them made into a bouquet.

DRINK IT IN
Once we nailed down the color and logo, the ideas for guest gifts started to flow. Stuff personalized mugs with tea and biscotti for a sweet treat.

The Friedman Factor:
STRIKE A POSE

At parties, guests of honor often get stuck in the same spot taking photos with people. So I had a cardboard cutout of myself made in the same dress I wore for the party. Guests had a blast posing with it and I was free to walk around and enjoy myself.

PRIMAL ELEMENTS

Rain Scent
Parfum d'Ondée

A clean scent of cool scented clean.

DIRTY TALK
Handmade soaps are an inexpensive way to show
guests some good, clean fun.

PETAL PUSHERS
Who doesn't love a beautiful bouquet? I filled one of my "shops" with gorgeous flowers that guests could pick out and have made into a bouquet wrapped with signature JLove tissue paper, of course!

BIRTHDAY BITES

When guests arrived for the party, models greeted them with tequila lime shots that had been individually poured down a JLove ice sculpture to make them cold. I also had someone sabering and pouring champagne. Creating a little theater near the door always gets guests in the mood.

The food was just as sexy

❉ Assorted cones filled with steak tartar, Dijon, and capers; Maine lobster with Serrano chiles, cucumber, and lime; salmon with red onion, dill, and lemon oil; tuna tartar with soy and wasabi

❉ Mini Kobe cheeseburgers with caramelized onions, aged cheddar, and fries

❉ Roast turkey breast slider with Dijon mayonnaise on a Parker House bun

❉ Rock shrimp with Sriracha chili sauce

❉ Oysters, mussels, spicy cocktail sauce, and remoulade

❉ An assortment of caviar with melba toast, potato pancakes, egg, onion, and crème fraiche

❉ Hand-carved beef tenderloin with Dijon mustard sauce and creamy horseradish

❉ Grilled baby lamb chops with rosemary and mint

❉ Lobster mashed potatoes

❉ Grilled asparagus

❉ Artisanal cheeses

❉ Orecchiette pasta with Parmesan cream chicken

❉ Italian rolls and breads

PRESENTATION IS EVERYTHING
Colored plates add pop and textured linens create visual interest that complements the beauty of the food.

get creative

GAME ON!
BUILDING YOUR OWN BOUTIQUE IS JUST ONE OF MANY PARTY POSSIBILITIES

Eye Candy: A model wearing a sweets-themed costume handed out JLove cookies at the party.

Here are a few more interactive ideas:

❋ My father loves betting, so for his eightieth birthday, I created a horserace at home. A company brought in machines; we placed bets and watched fabricated races on our TV together, cheering our horses on.

❋ Do a *Family Feud* party: create teams, your own questions, and a grand prize. Bonus points for hiring a production company to create a set just like the '70s game show.

❋ My youngest daughter, Taylor, loves to cook and bake. For her eighteenth birthday, I hired the chef at the Joule, a boutique hotel in Dallas, to give her and her girlfriends a cooking lesson. They put on aprons and clogs and got their hands into everything from sushi and small pizzas to stir-fry. They even learned how to decorate a cake. Afterward they ate the food they made and took the cakes home as party favors.

BEST BUDS
Made of green orchids, this mannequin piqued guests' interest at the doll shop, where my girlfriends picked out fashions that would make Chanel jealous.

love and laughter

VALENTINE'S DAY

In most relationships, romance starts the fire but laughter is what sustains a couple over the long haul. It keeps you young, connected, and coming back for more.

The best Valentine's Day parties follow the same suit: they start sexy and intimate and end with lots of giggles and grins. And if it gets a tad risqué, it'll make it even more memorable.

Dinner for two is nice, but you can do that any Saturday night. Unlike so many other holidays, Valentine's Day isn't bound by tradition. So shake it up and put some real love and laughter into this Hallmark holiday.

I wanted the invitation to say "sexy," so I had a clear acrylic tray wrapped with gold and red ribbon. Inside, the invitation rested on a gold pillow. The box on top held red chocolate kisses and was gilded with gold and jewels.

FEELING THORNY
Red is the color of passion. Accent your table with small, low arrangements of red roses and scatter petals around the place settings.

TABLE TALK
The key to an interesting table is mixing elements and steering clear of being too matchy matchy. Layer metal, glass, gold and silver so the table has depth and dimension.

LABOR OF LOVE

SO INVITING

The guest list for a Valentine's Day party is best kept small, so do something special for the invitation. Pair them with a box of artisan chocolates or bottle of wine or champagne and have them hand delivered.

HEART OF THE MATTER

Everyone expects red roses—in vases, scattered across the table, and stacked in small vases. No one expects a giant heart to be installed on the front lawn. Call a local set design or production company to shop sizes and styles. Have guests pose underneath it for a photo when they arrive, and send it to them in a frame later as a thank-you.

HOUSEHOLD NAMES

Valentine's Day is the perfect time to have fun with place settings. Mix dark and light pinks or reds with gold and silver. Instead of place cards, write each couple's name on a heart—*Janelle Loves Larry; Larry Loves Janelle*—or have a silhouette cut of each couple kissing and do an overlay of their names on top.

FOREPLAY

Put your heart into it: serve heart-shaped butter with bread or heart-shaped blinis with caviar. Buy a small stack of linen napkins and write fun sayings on them in red marker, then pass them out with appetizers and cocktails.

Too sophisticated for shots? Serve what I call "onesies," or airplane bottles of vodka. They are irresistible with a red, bendy straw poking out of the top.

Color coordinated clothing adds to the look of love.

Heart-shaped blinis topped with caviar pair well with an airline bottle of vodka and bendy red straw.

BLESS YOUR HEART
Before the food arrives, the plate is a perfect place to make a statement.

Jodi
Loves
Jerry

MENU INSPIRATION

Amuse Bouche
* Pheasant under glass

Appetizer
* Seared sea scallop on purple cauliflower puree with blood orange beurre blanc and hearts of fire salad

Salad
Heart to heart
* Baby romaine hearts and hearts of palm salad with shaved fennel and pommery mustard vinaigrette

Intermezzo
* Pink grapefruit champagne sorbet

Main Course
Choice of:
Hearts and Sole
* George's Bank lemon sole and poached globe artichoke hearts with Japanese plum and shitake mushroom broth plus crispy purple sweet potato chips
  or
* Yoakum Texas Wagyu filet mignon on pommes puree

Cheese Plate Shared by Two
* Purple Haze from Cypress Grove Farms in Sonoma, California
* California Chevre from Caprino Royale in Waco, Texas

Dessert
* Chocolate cherry ice cream heart sandwich with mallow fluff and cherry jam
* Vanilla custard shooter with passion fruit orange sauce
* Mignardises chocolate shots filled with after-dinner cordials and cognacs
* Petite heart-shaped cookies

The Friedman Factor:

ROYAL TREATMENT

I never tell guests about the entertainment because I want it to be a surprise. That night, a pianist played romantic music during dinner and Mosaic, an all-male a cappella group, was set to sing a few songs afterward, but I wanted dessert to be memorable.

I'd had delicious pie at a local bakery and it sparked the idea to serve heart-shaped ice cream sandwiches then have whole pies in every flavor wheeled in and served from a rolling cart. Even when I rented a gorgeous glass cart, the presentation didn't feel like enough. And then it hit me: I'd have drag queens come in and serve those pies with a side of sass.

It was so much better than I'd imagined: the "Reddi-wip Girls" were a blast. They told jokes, sat on guests' laps, and served those pies in style. Everyone laughed so hard and could not believe what they'd just seen in my dining room.

NAME THAT TUNE

Hired entertainers aren't the only ones who love to perform—guests enjoy getting in on the action after a fun night (and a few cocktails!). Go around the table and sing "The Name Game," the rhyming song that rose to popularity in the 1960s:

Larry Larry bo berry, banana fana for ferry, fe fi mo merry . . . Larry!

ANNIVERSARY PARTIES

Whether you're toasting each other or renewing vows, write down what you want to say so you don't forget it in the moment.

When Larry proposed to me years ago, he said, "I can't promise you everything, but I can promise you never a dull moment." Believe me: he kept that promise. So when we celebrated two decades of marriage, I decided to return the favor with an anniversary party that accomplished the same mission. It was our way of thanking all the friends and family who've supported us over the years.

Whether you throw one for yourself or someone else, remember to put love in every detail. Anyone can serve food and schedule entertainment, but love is contagious and inspiring and turns a good party into a memorable event.

MAKE A SCENE
With a little imagination, a hotel ballroom can become a nightclub. This sexy space was the backdrop for a personal concert by Brian McKnight.

MEAL TO REMEMBER
With a few personal touches, a restaurant dining room can be a special space to share a meal with family and friends.

EVERYONE LOVES TO BE ROMANCED

MAKE A MOVE

When scoping out spaces, look for ways to move guests around so they're not sitting in one spot all night—like a hotel restaurant with a nearby ballroom or event space.

Even when I entertain at home, I like to keep the flow going by having appetizers on the deck before guests sit at the table for a few hours. People get bored being confined to one room and it gives them the chance to wrap up conversations and start new ones with different people.

PEAR UP!

Send a little something to let guests know they're part of the party. I had the idea to send a silk box with two Baccarat crystal pears inside and an invitation that said, "the perfect pair." The man who delivered them presented each box with a rose and asked the guest if they would accept the rose. Everyone loves to be romanced.

STAMPS OF APPROVAL

Find a great old photo of the couple and use it to create a stamp for the invitation. It's an extra detail that turns a plain envelope into an attraction.

I've done branded stamps for everything from charity events to retirement parties and personal correspondence. Pretty much everything except bills. Neiman Marcus doesn't need my personal stamp!

PICTURE THIS

Do something special with the menu card. Have it set inside an envelope with a photo of the couple on the front and the marriage date or special quote. For couples married thirty-plus years, an old wedding photo—or then-and-now pictures—gets guests oohing and aahing.

The crystal pears from our invitation turned into keepsakes. I love seeing them in everyone's china cabinets when I visit.

DISH IT OUT
Give guests the menu and schedule so they can relax and enjoy the evening.

I could not have known
before we met that
every step in my life
would lead me to you.

Ed Bates
LOVELY EVENING

TO TOAST OR NOT TO TOAST

Toasts are a personal pet peeve. Once someone starts, others feel obligated to follow suit and it can really bog down the energy you worked so hard to create. Here are a few ways to work around it:

* Make a note of it on the invitation so guests won't take the time to prepare one. Also include a line at the bottom of the menu card as a reminder. Something simple like "No toasts, please" gets the message across.

* For my daughter's rehearsal dinner, we asked guests to send a short video toast and we combined them into one video that we played that evening. That way we could control the timing.

* Toast yourself: For our anniversary party, Larry and I got up, spoke about each other and talked a little about what kept us together for twenty years. It's a nice alternative to renewing vows.

REEL LIFE

Everyone loves looking at photos of the couple throughout the years. It's fun and brings a sweet, emotional element to the evening. Months in advance, collect images of the couple from family and friends and have them put to music in a video. Larry surprised me with one and everyone cracked up at my lifetime of hairdos.

BRIGHT IDEA
Add your initial to lanterns, globes, or other lighting to up the wow factor when guests arrive.

MENU INSPIRATION

Crab ravioli

❋ Hen of the woods mushrooms, brown butter, hazelnut

Baby red oak and duck salad

❋ Pickled shallots, brioche croutons

Entrée: choice of one

❋ Lentil-crusted Scottish salmon

❋ Butter-braised lobster

❋ Caramelized pheasant

❋ Bison ribeye

Dessert: choice of one

❋ Plum cobbler with cinnamon almond crust

❋ Chocolate peanut butter bar

❋ Dark chocolate cake

❋ Chocolate napoleon

EGG THEM ON
Treat guests to a caviar bar with
all the accoutrements.

Janelle's Famous Flourless Chocolate Torte

2 (8 ounce) packages semisweet chocolate squares, coarsely chopped
½ cup butter
5 large eggs separated
1 tablespoon vanilla extract
¼ cup sugar
Unsweetened cocoa for dusting

1. Grease a 9-inch springform pan and dust it with the unsweetened cocoa.

2. Melt chopped chocolate and butter in a saucepan over low heat, stirring until smooth.

3. Whisk together egg yolks and vanilla in large bowl, gradually stir in chocolate mixture. Whisk until well blended.

4. Beat egg whites at high speed with an electric mixer until soft peaks form. Gradually add sugar, until sugar dissolves and still has soft peaks. Fold ⅓ beaten egg white mixture into chocolate mixture, gently fold the rest of the egg white mixture until blended.

5. Spoon batter into prepared pan.

6. Bake 375 degrees 25 minutes (do not overbake).

7. Let stand 10 minutes before removing sides of pan.

Top with blueberries or strawberries and a side of whipped cream.

The Friedman Factor:
SWEET SEND-OFF

Shortly after my parents got married, my mother gave my father ptomaine poisoning because she didn't know how to cook. She asked my dad's aunt Celia, who was an unbelievable cook, for help and turned into a tremendous force in the kitchen with five children following her around.

Cooking for someone is one of the top ways we show love. And food makes an excellent edible party favor. Send guests home with a bag of homemade granola, a bottle of Bloody Mary mix for a "morning after" cocktail, or try this gluten-free torte, which I've given out at the end of many events.

If you have to get your hands dirty planning a party, they may as well be covered in chocolate.

This heart-and-arrow appetizer was made of red and black caviar.

THE GOOD GUEST

One of the many benefits of hosting events is that it makes you a more sympathetic guest at someone else's party. Here's what I've learned from years spent sitting on both sides of the table:

TABLE TALK

* If you're seated next to people you don't know, ask questions. Everyone has a story and knows something you don't.

* Avoid politics unless you're in a like-minded group or with those who can have healthy discussions about it. If you're not sure, pick another topic.

* Never bring a cell phone to the table.

DON'T OFFER THE HOST SUGGESTIONS ON WAYS TO MAKE THE PARTY BETTER NEXT TIME.

* Never bring a child unless they're invited.

* Drink in moderation. The difference between a happy guest and a sloppy guest is about two cocktails.

THE RSVP

* Always RSVP—the sooner the better. If factors beyond your control prevent you from making a decision, call the host and let them know you'll respond as soon as possible.

* If you RSVP yes, you absolutely must attend unless it's an emergency situation. It's rude to call at the last minute or not show up at all.

THE HOSTESS GIFT

* If the party is being held at home, take a small gift—but not anything that creates work for the hostess or intrudes on the evening. For example, flowers seem like an easy gift, but the hostess might have had floral arrangements made for the party or not have any vases on hand. Flowers are best sent the day after the party as a thank-you.

* A personal gift for the wife—instead of something for the house—says so much about gratitude. If the host is someone I know, I'll buy something personal, like a scarf or new lipstick color.

* Never take wine. Wine says, "Oh, I just pulled this off my shelf without any thought or care." Try gourmet olive oils or cheeses—something that says you put effort into it.

COOL IDEA
Kick off the night with an ice sculpture and signature cocktail.

make faith beautiful

CELEBRATING JEWISH HOLIDAYS

chapter 9

Statement pieces can be multipurpose. These gold crown boxes are used to serve red beet horseradish for Passover seder and Mediterranean spreads at other dinner parties throughout the year.

In the broad sense, faith is part of any event. You can work and schedule, sample and plan (and plan, and plan), but eventually you have to let go and trust that things will happen exactly as they should.

When faith is the focus of an event, traditions take precedence. It's what binds us to our religion and family. But that doesn't mean every Passover seder or bat mitzvah has to look and feel exactly the same. The trick is to honor the customs and get creative with everything else, showing equal respect to the old and new.

CUSTOM-MADE
From the flowers and vases to the linens and silverware, every piece on the Passover table has special significance.

PASSOVER

Create a Time Capsule

In my family, we all share the responsibility of hosting holidays. Passover is mine. Many years ago, my sister-in-law Helen's parents, Ronnie and Nancy Horowitz, started a tradition that I've continued. After our seder is completed, I hand everyone a pen and each person writes anything they want in the seder book. It's so much fun to go back through the years, see who joined us and what they said. It's become a little time capsule that reinforces the importance of family and our history together.

Tradition with a Twist

Years ago, when Larry and I chaired the Jewish Federation of Dallas's one hundredth anniversary event, we hired an African American choir to learn and sing Hebrew songs. It was an unexpected touch that made such an impact on the guests. A few years later, I wanted to do something special for my sister-in-law Helen, who was diagnosed with ovarian cancer, so I hired the choir again to sing Jewish prayers at Passover. It was beautiful and meant a lot to everyone.

THE RITE THING
Setting the table for Passover takes time and attention. Everything must be in its place—seder plates, matzo, salt water, place cards, and programs—so that the service can begin and end without interruption.

MENU INSPIRATION

Passover Seder

❖ Appetizers served in the family room

❖ Traditional Chopped Liver
with Parsley Garnish

❖ Matzo Crackers

❖ Egg White Salad and Egg Yolk Salad
with Matzo Crisps

❖ Matzo Pizzas

❖ Classic Hummus

❖ Olive Hummus

❖ Carrots, Celery, and Cucumber

❖ Matzo Pita

Dinner Menu

❖ Matzo Cracker Place Cards

❖ Decanted Red and White Wines

EACH SEDER PLATE TO INCLUDE:

❖ Freshly Grated Beet Horseradish

❖ Roasted Egg

❖ Lamb Shank

❖ Parsley

❖ Salt Water and Chorosis

THE FOLLOWING SERVED:

❖ Nonnie's Matzo Ball Soup

❖ Oval-Shaped Quenelles of Gefilte Fish

❖ Romaine Leaf and Carrot Coins

❖ Pickled Beet Horseradish

THE FOLLOWING SERVED FROM
THE BUFFET:

❖ Large and Cherry Heirloom Tomato
and Dallas Mozzarella Salad

❖ Baby Basil

❖ Twenty-Five-Year-Aged
Balsamic Drizzle

❖ Pesto

❖ Baby Romaine with Fresh Hearts
of Palm and Tomato

❖ Cilantro Lime Vinaigrette

❖ Side of Salmon

❖ Roasted and Served with
Capers, Lemon, and Olive Oil

❖ Apricot and Preserved
Lemon-Braised Chicken

❖ Salt-Roasted Fingerling Potatoes
with Fresh Herbs

ROASTED BABY ROOT VEGETABLES
TO INCLUDE:

❖ Beets, Carrots, Turnips Tossed with
Lemon Thyme and Olive Oil

❖ Wild Mushroom and Tricolored
Asparagus Sauté

Dessert Buffet

❖ French Macarons

❖ Macaroons with Dark Chocolate

❖ Flourless Chocolate Cake

❖ Almond Pineapple Cake

❖ Chocolate Matzo

❖ Fresh Berries and Melons

HOLIDAY HELPINGS
Served in bold-colored pedestal bowls, charoset is a
sweet, dark-colored paste made of nuts.

The Friedman Factor:

UNLEAVENED LEVITY

∙ ∙ ∙ The tabletop is a perfect place to inject a little whimsy and matzo name cards are a showstopper. Fill a pastry bag with melted chocolate—you can also use a sandwich bag and cut off the tip—and write each guest's name on a large piece of matzo. Let cool and dry, then prop it up in front of their plate for a fun name plate that doubles as dessert!

IT'S ABOUT TIME

Every event I do, whether it's a Passover seder for thirty or a charity gala for one thousand, has its own timeline. Taking the time to walk through each part of the evening on paper helps me visualize and notice pitfalls, and is an essential part of making everything go smoothly.

Here's a sample of one from a Chanukah party I held at my home:

Friedman Family Chanukah Party

SUNDAY, DECEMBER 16
Table set up at 4 p.m.
(For a holiday party, I always set my tables a few days in advance. That way, if I need something extra, I have time to get it before the party.)

FRIDAY, DECEMBER 21

4 p.m.	Set up
	Dining table set with eight candles
	Seating for ten plus one high chair and one booster
	Game boards and gifts set for each guest
	Cover floor in garage and catering kitchen prior to chef arrival
4:30 p.m.	Chef arrives with culinary staff
6 p.m.	Kitchen prepares two meals for housekeepers
6:30 p.m.	Musicians arrive
6:30 p.m.	All arrangements complete
7 p.m.	Family arrives
	Drinks and hors d'oeuvres with chef in kitchen
7:45 p.m.	Seated for first course
	Salads served
	Dessert served
8:30 p.m.	Family game begins
	Some gifts distributed
	Kitchen staff cleans up and departs
9:30 p.m.	More gifts (housekeepers to assist with wrapping paper)
10 p.m.	Trash removed from home
10:30 p.m.	Cleanup complete

LIGHT THE WAY
Though Passover is steeped in tradition, tabletop touches like a new, artistic menorah connect the past with the present.

HELPING THE HELP

I love to cook, but I often hire caterers for in-home events so I can spend less time in the kitchen and more time with guests. This means making house rules for staff as clear as possible:

 ❋ Before entering the kitchen, make sure all shoes are clean.

 ❋ Do not put anything in the disposal that doesn't belong there.

 ❋ Make sure all ovens are turned off.

 ❋ Clean all surfaces.

 ❋ Remove all trash from property.

 ❋ Do not pour or drag anything outside.

When I host an event at a restaurant or hotel, I always sit down with the maître d' to set my service expectations so he or she can communicate them to the servers:

 ❋ At least one server per table.

 ❋ Be attentive to guests.

 ❋ Promptly pick up dirty glasses and dishes.

 ❋ All food must be served at the table at the same time so guests can eat at the same time.

 ❋ Servers should offer refills of drinks.

BAT MITZVAHS

SPREAD IT OUT

Six children means six bar and bat mitzvahs, so I was a pro by the time my youngest child, Taylor, turned twelve. Children's parties are much different than adult parties: children don't want to stand around and chitchat and they aren't content to sit and relax. They want constant activity and entertainment.

activity and entertainment

DREAM UP A THEME

Taylor's bat mitzvah was a two-day event: the first night we did the religious ritual with a dessert party afterward and the next night we hosted a party for her friends and ours. It requires more time, effort, and financial investment, but we wanted to give equal attention to the ceremony and celebration.

MAZEL TOV . . . AND ALOHA!

We knew Taylor's party was going to have a lot of moving parts—music, dancing, food—so we chose a theme to create cohesiveness. We were doing annual family vacations in Hawaii at the time and went with that motif because there's so much you can do with it for any children's party:

※ Make a hula girl table! Have a table made with just enough space in the middle for a person to stand in and make sure it comes to waist height. Cover it with fake grass to look like a hula skirt and put leis on top. Set it by the entrance, put a girl in the middle, and have her hand out leis to guests as they arrive.

※ Do a tiki bar filled with fun things for kids to do: temporary tattoos, games, caricatures, and fun favors that can be personalized on the spot.

※ Set up a tent for dancing and have sea creatures projected onto the sides like you're in the ocean.

※ For favors, buy acrylic fish bowls and hand-paint each guest's name on it. Give them out at the end of the night with goldfish in baggies, some starter food, and care instructions.

※ For the kids' table, get a green, grass-like carpet and a low table so they can sit on the floor. Do a buffet of pizza, chicken fingers, burgers, and fries; food served in courses takes too long for their attention spans.

I even had a chair made to look like a shell and hired dancers to carry Taylor in and perform a choreographed routine with her as the star.

These hula dancers were the real deal flown in from Hawaii to entertain.

The teen room was set up like a tiki hut where the kids could eat, talk, and play games while the adults had a seated dinner.

Make an entrance! Taylor arrived in a custom seashell carried by professional models.

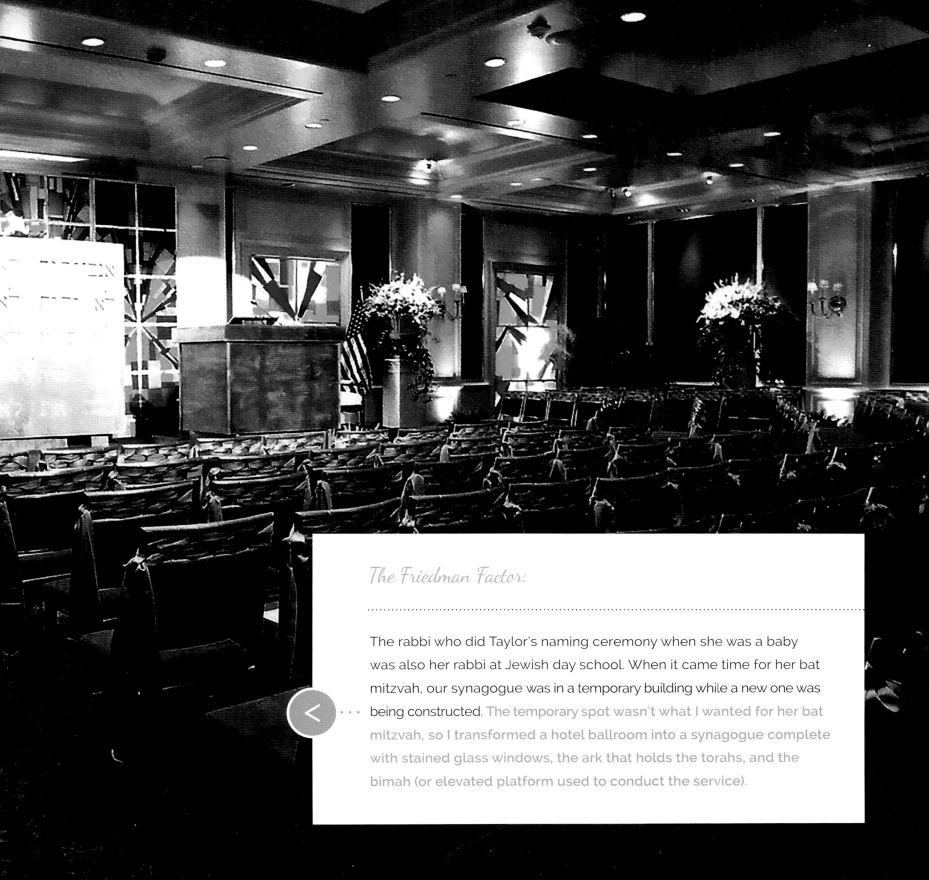

The Friedman Factor:

....

The rabbi who did Taylor's naming ceremony when she was a baby was also her rabbi at Jewish day school. When it came time for her bat mitzvah, our synagogue was in a temporary building while a new one was being constructed. The temporary spot wasn't what I wanted for her bat mitzvah, so I transformed a hotel ballroom into a synagogue complete with stained glass windows, the ark that holds the torahs, and the bimah (or elevated platform used to conduct the service).